Amazing Animals

Designs to Inspire Your Creative Genius

Published by Global Insight Productions in 2015

Illustration and Design Ewelina Terczynska
copyright 2015

BeHappyColoringBooks.com

ISBN 9780979694233

Join Our Creative Community
BeHappyColoringBooks.com

For your coloring and painting pleasure,
if you have creative genius ideas that you
would like for our artist to design, let us know.

We also want you to be a part of our Be Happy
Art Gallery. So go ahead and send us your
masterpiece and we will share it with the world.

You can contact us at **info@behappycoloring.com**

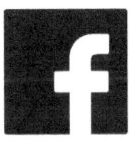 facebook.com/behappycoloring

 pinterest.com/behappycoloring

 Instagram.com/behappycoloring

 twitter.com/behappycoloring

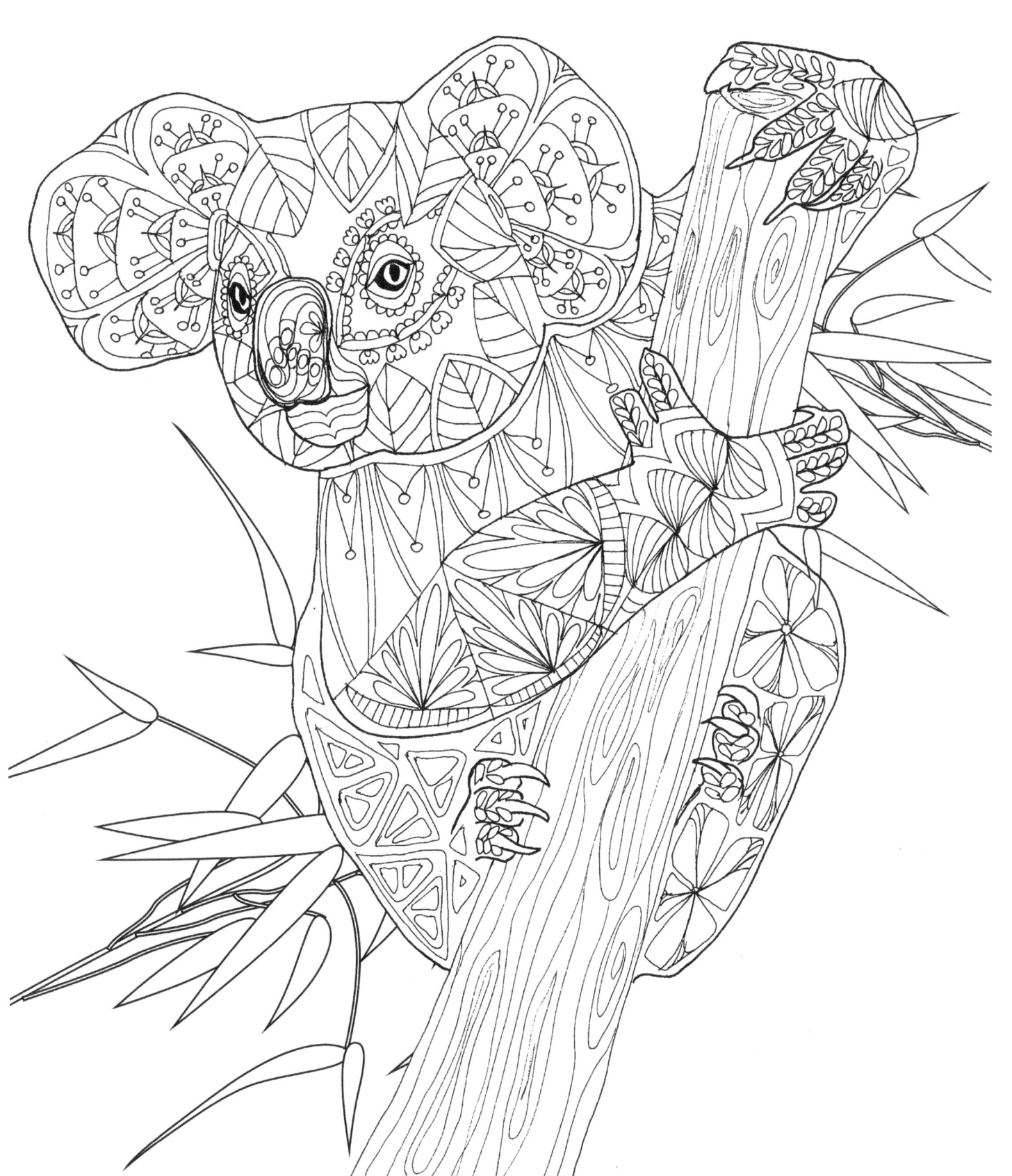

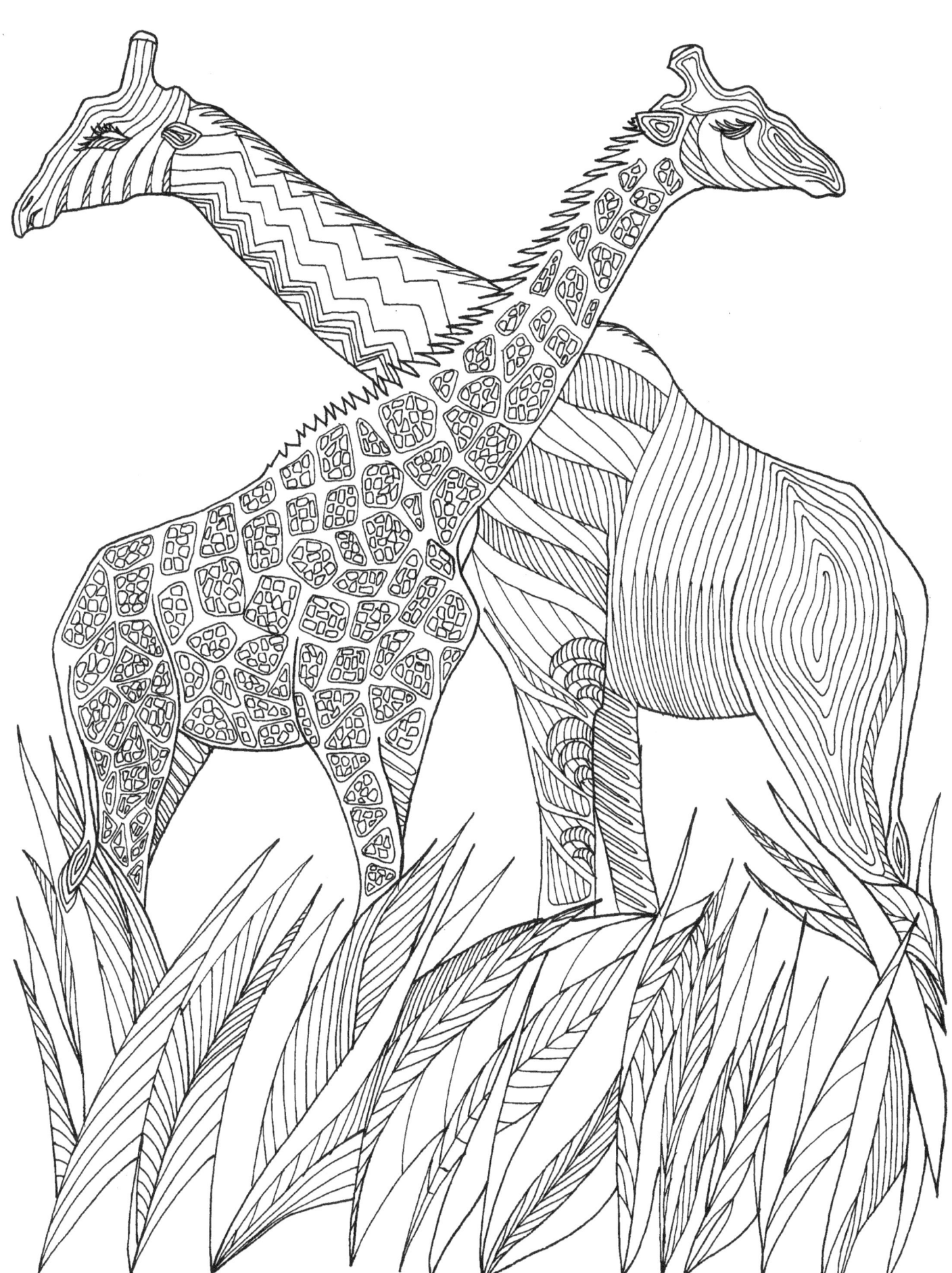

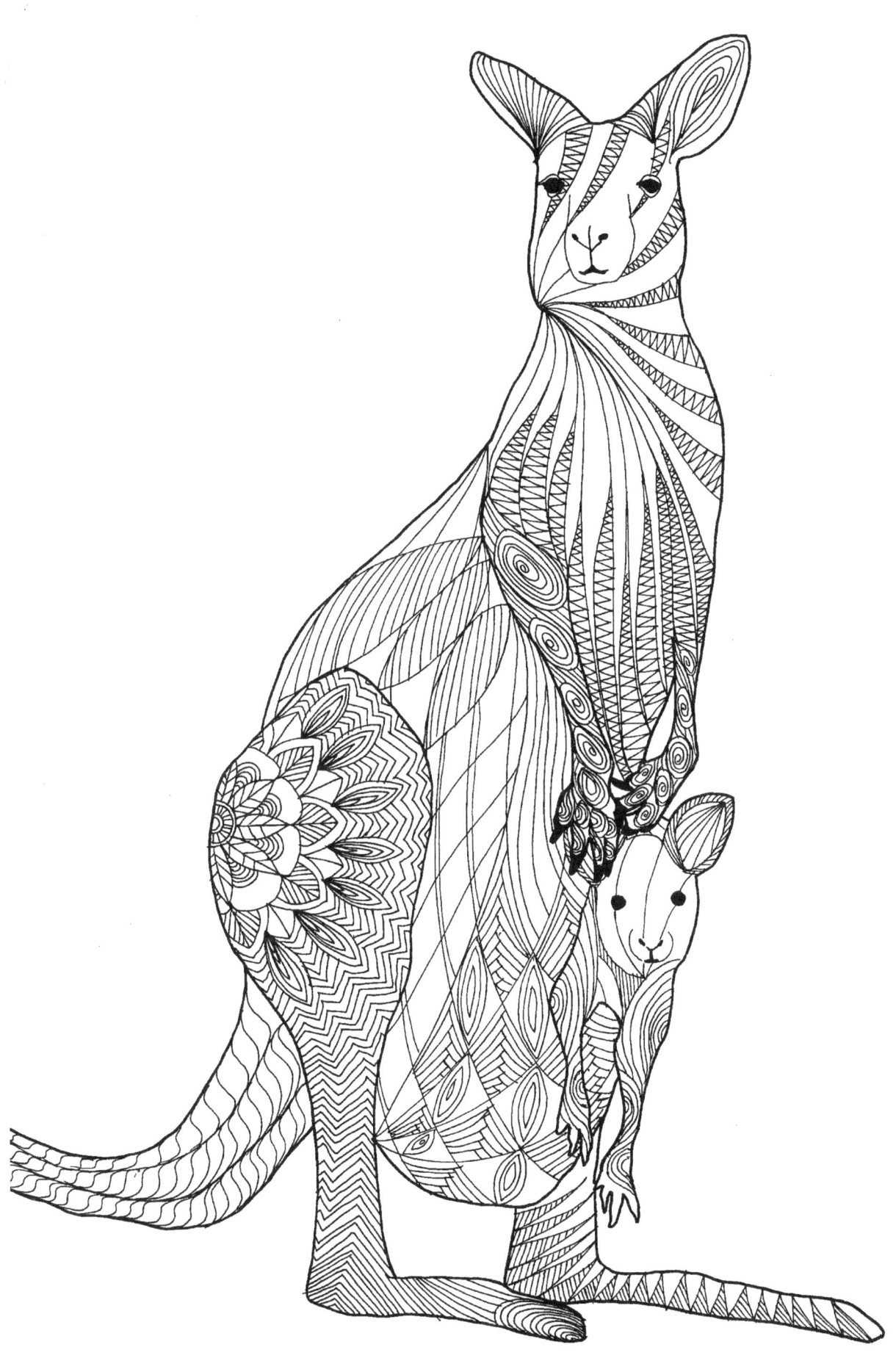

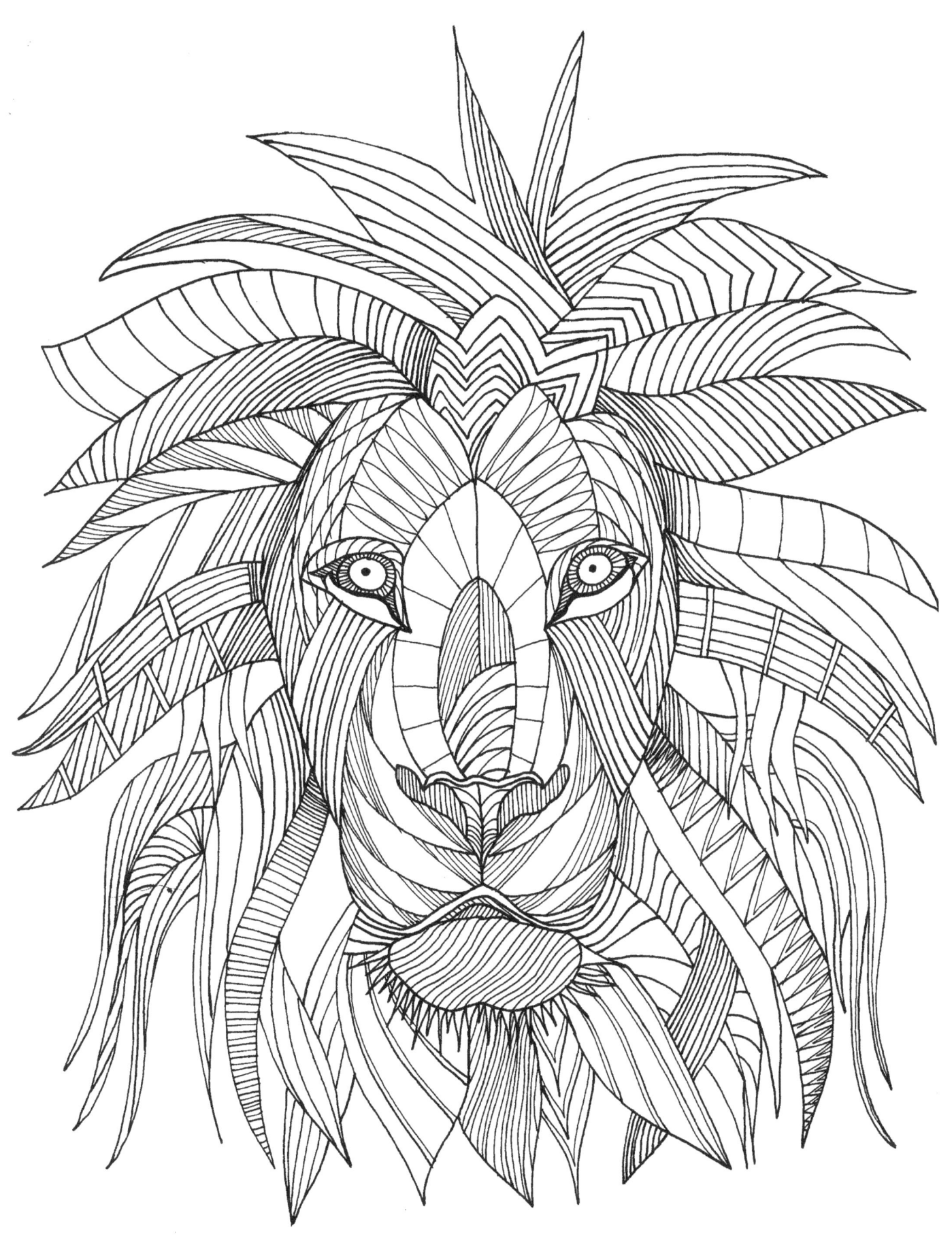

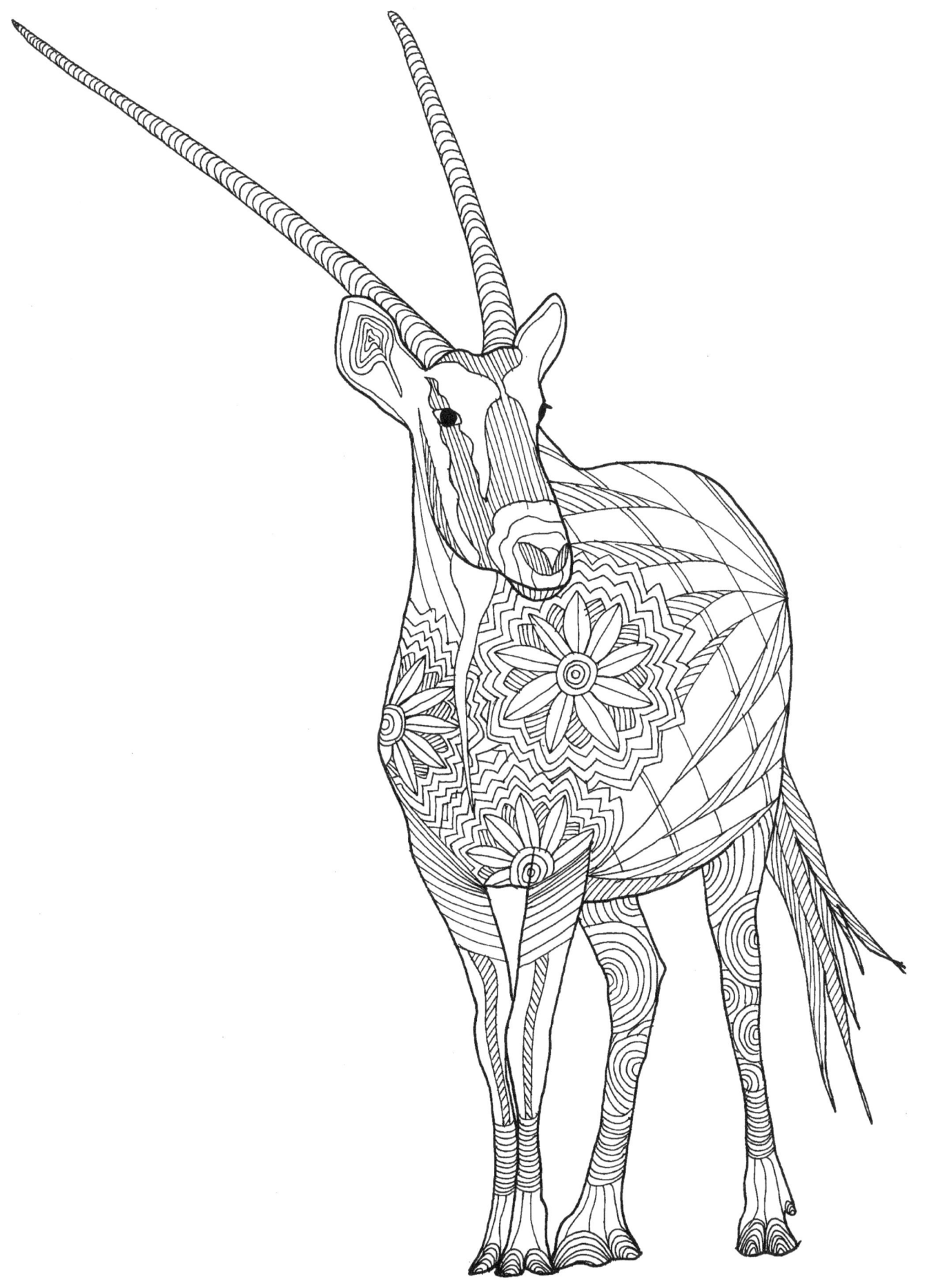

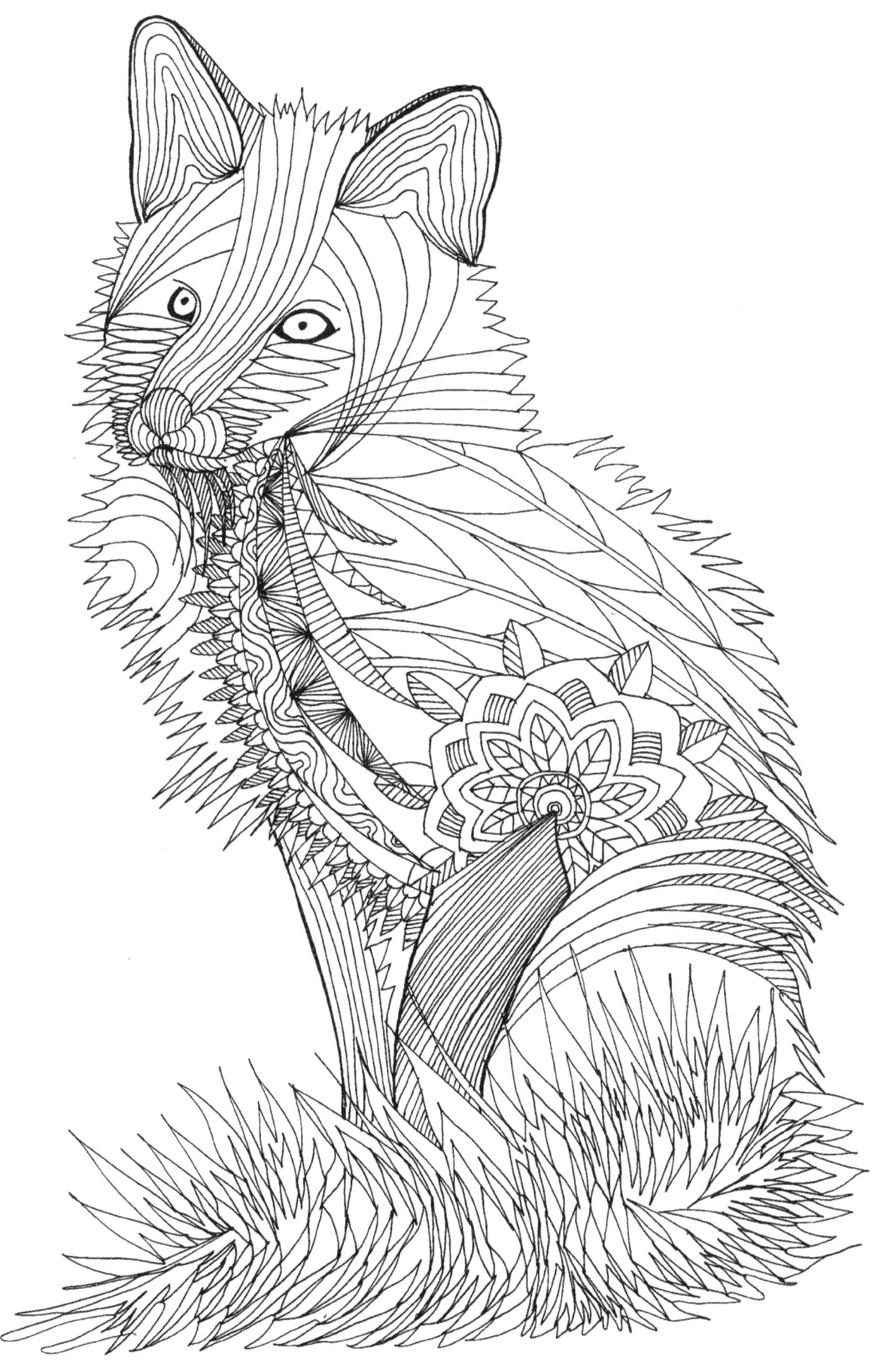

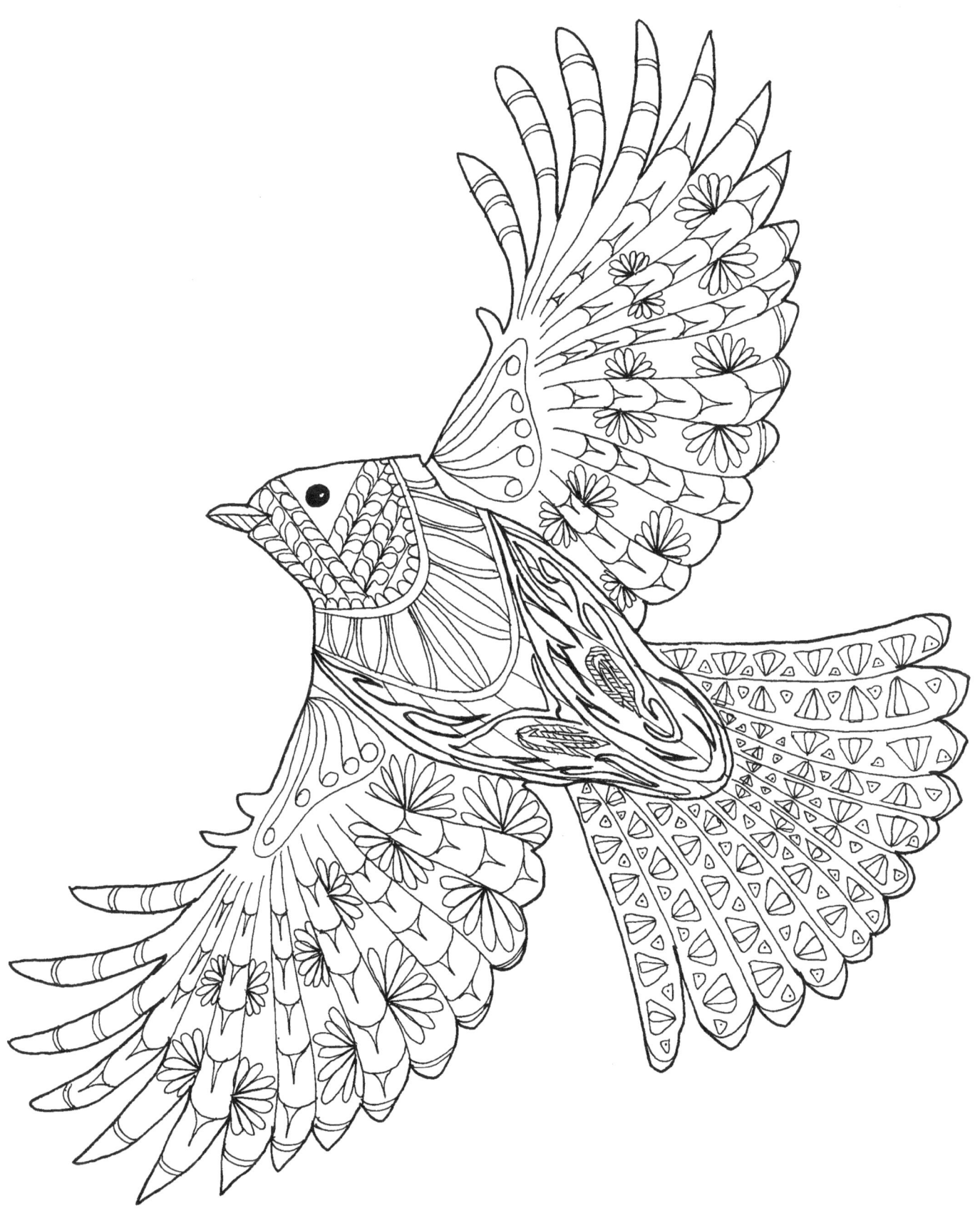

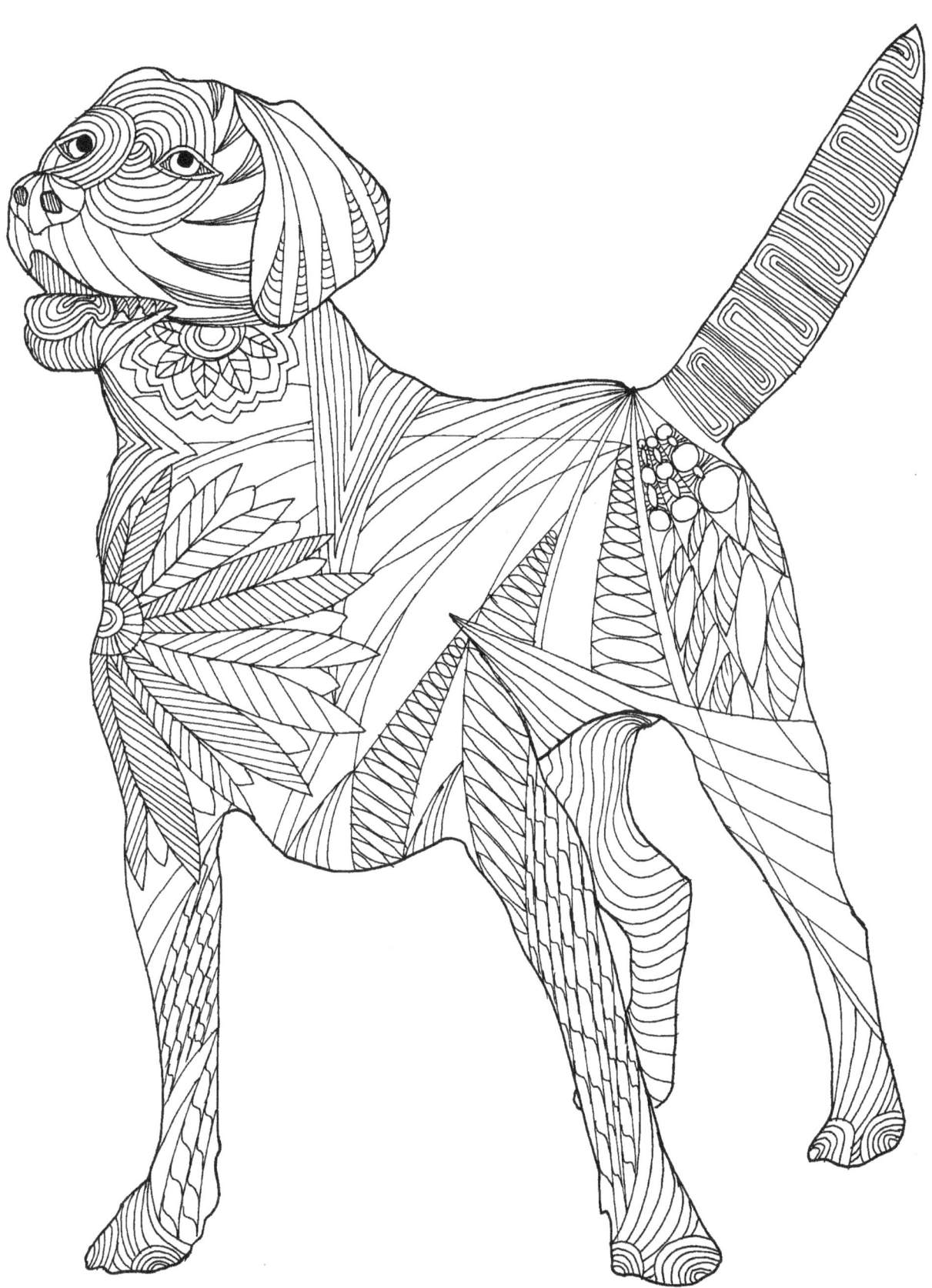

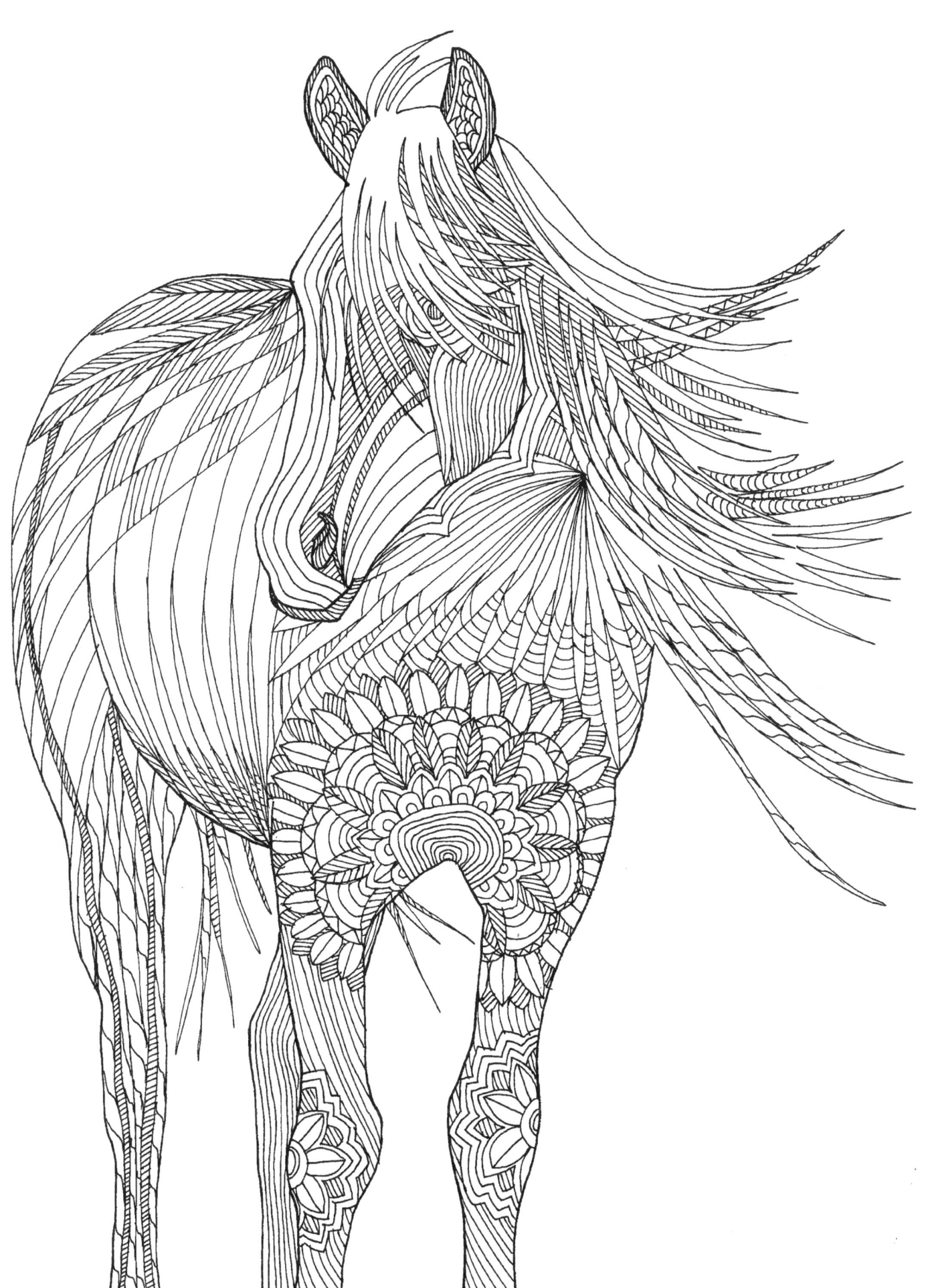

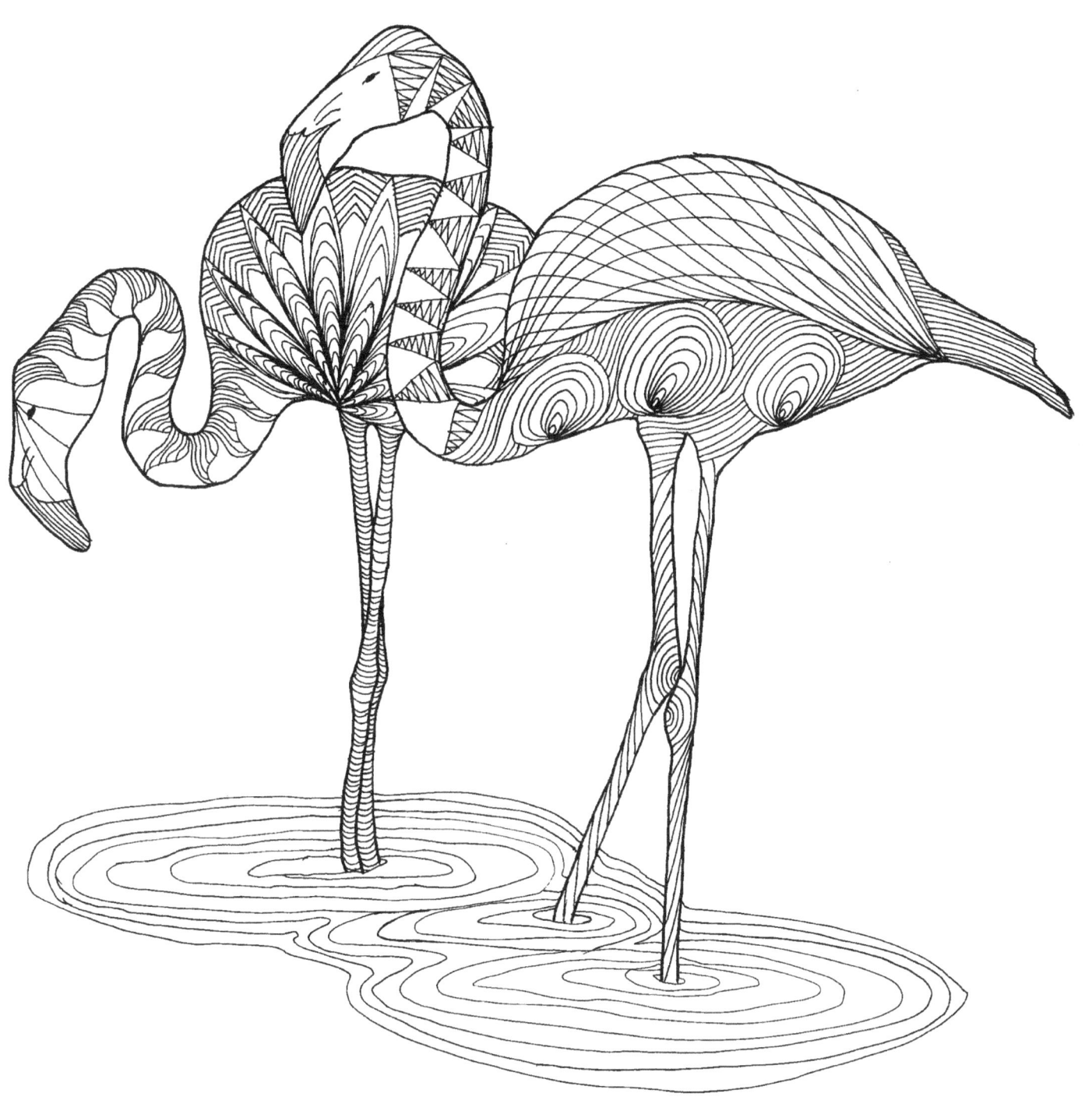

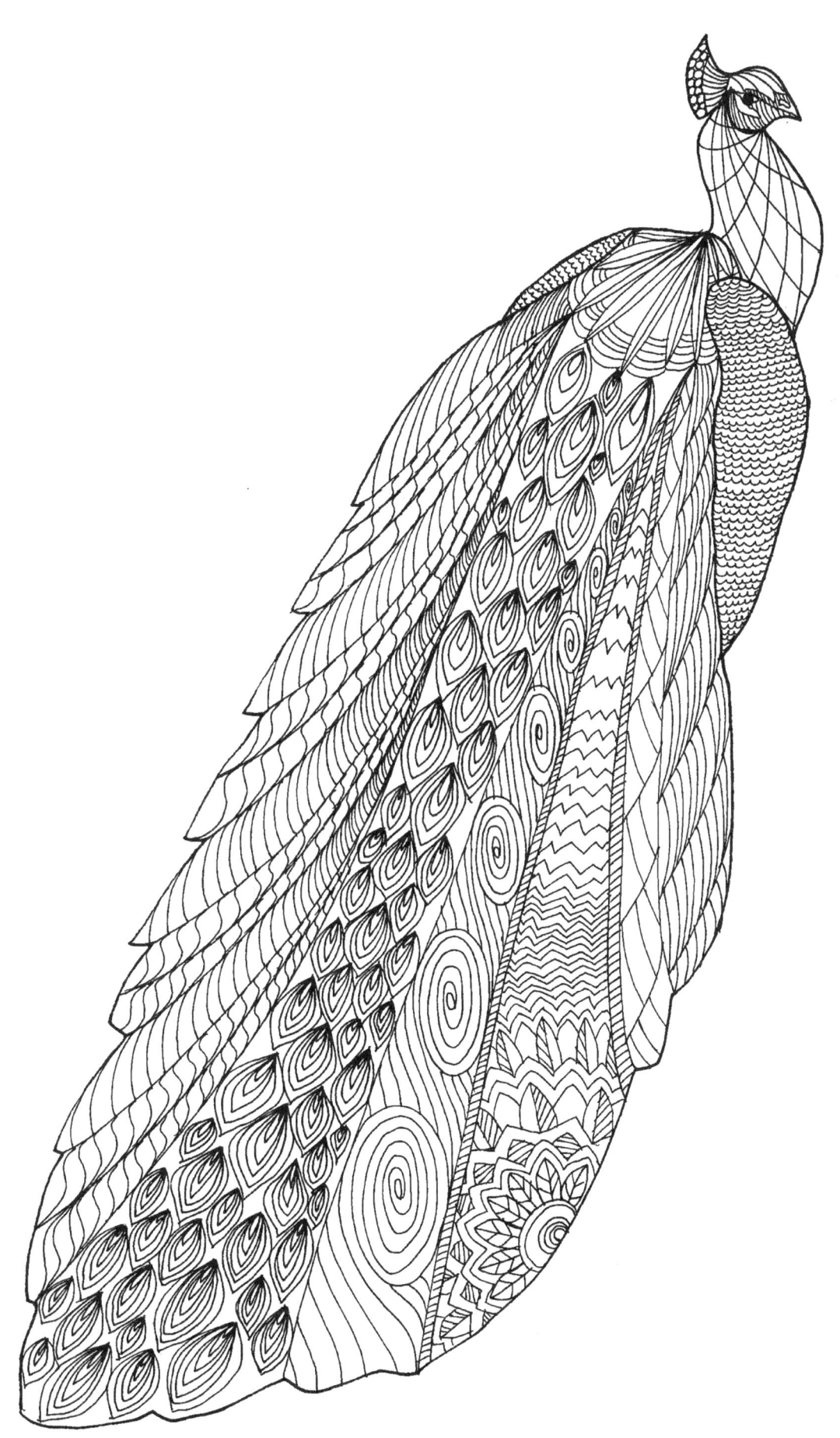

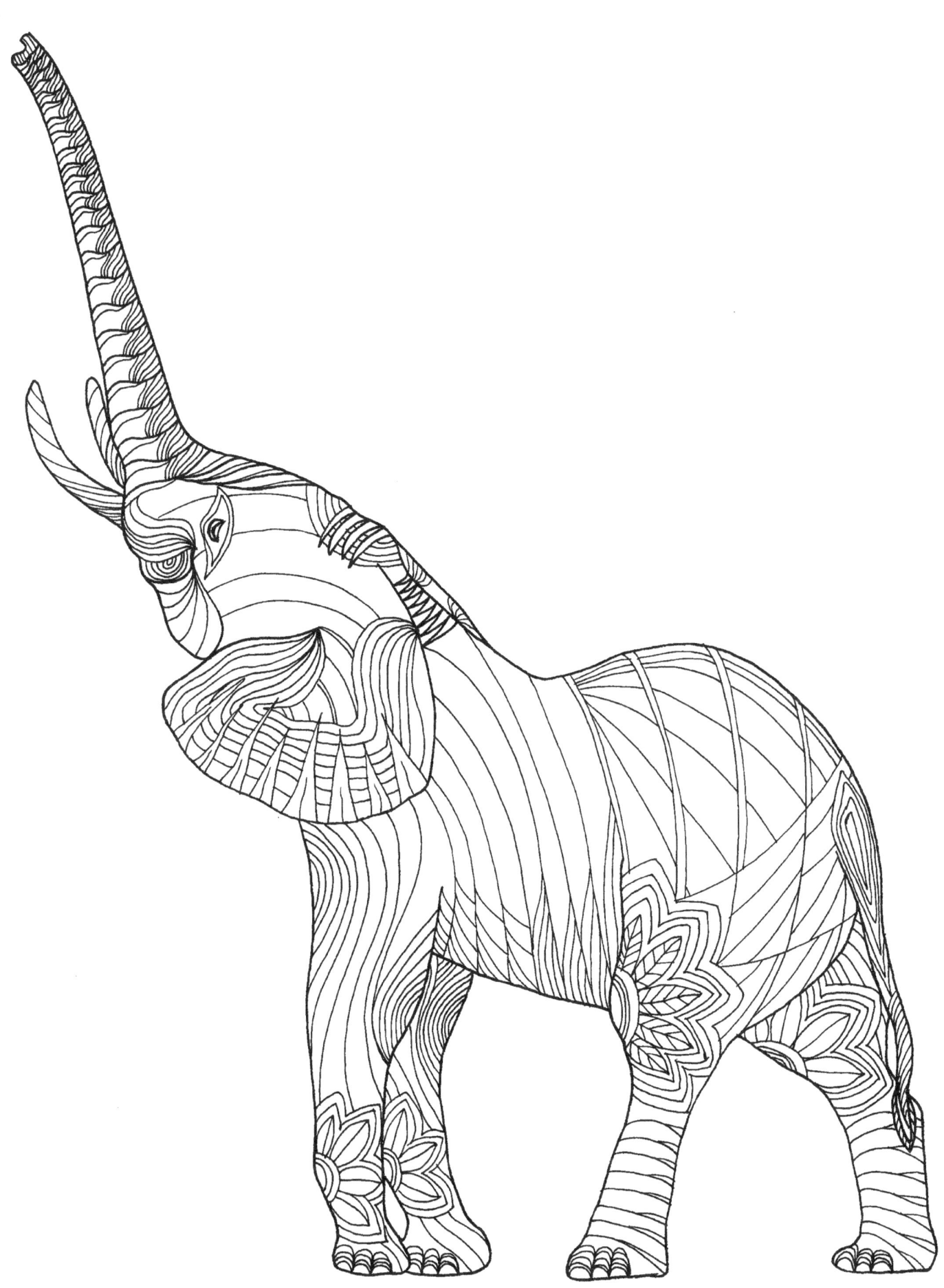

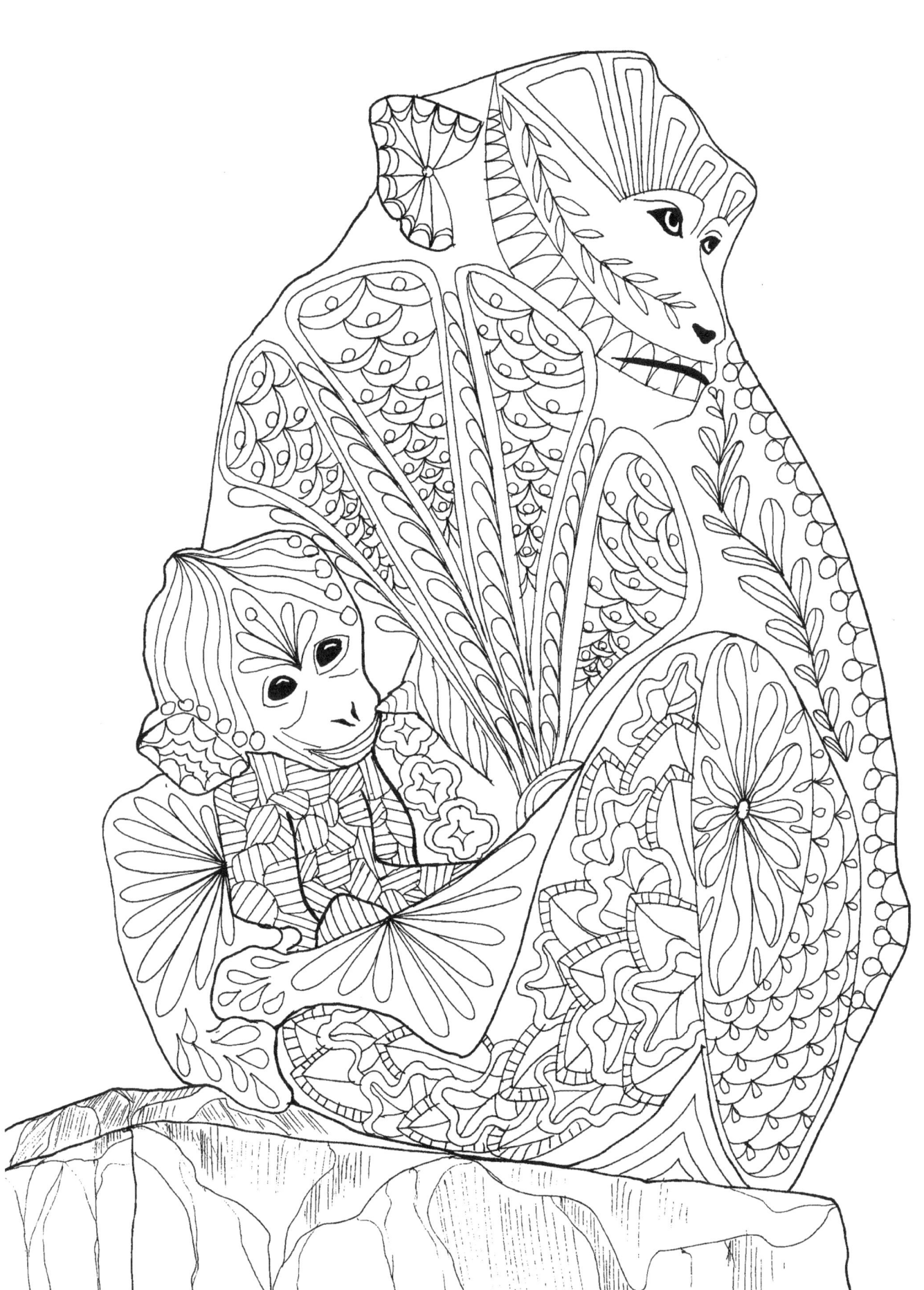

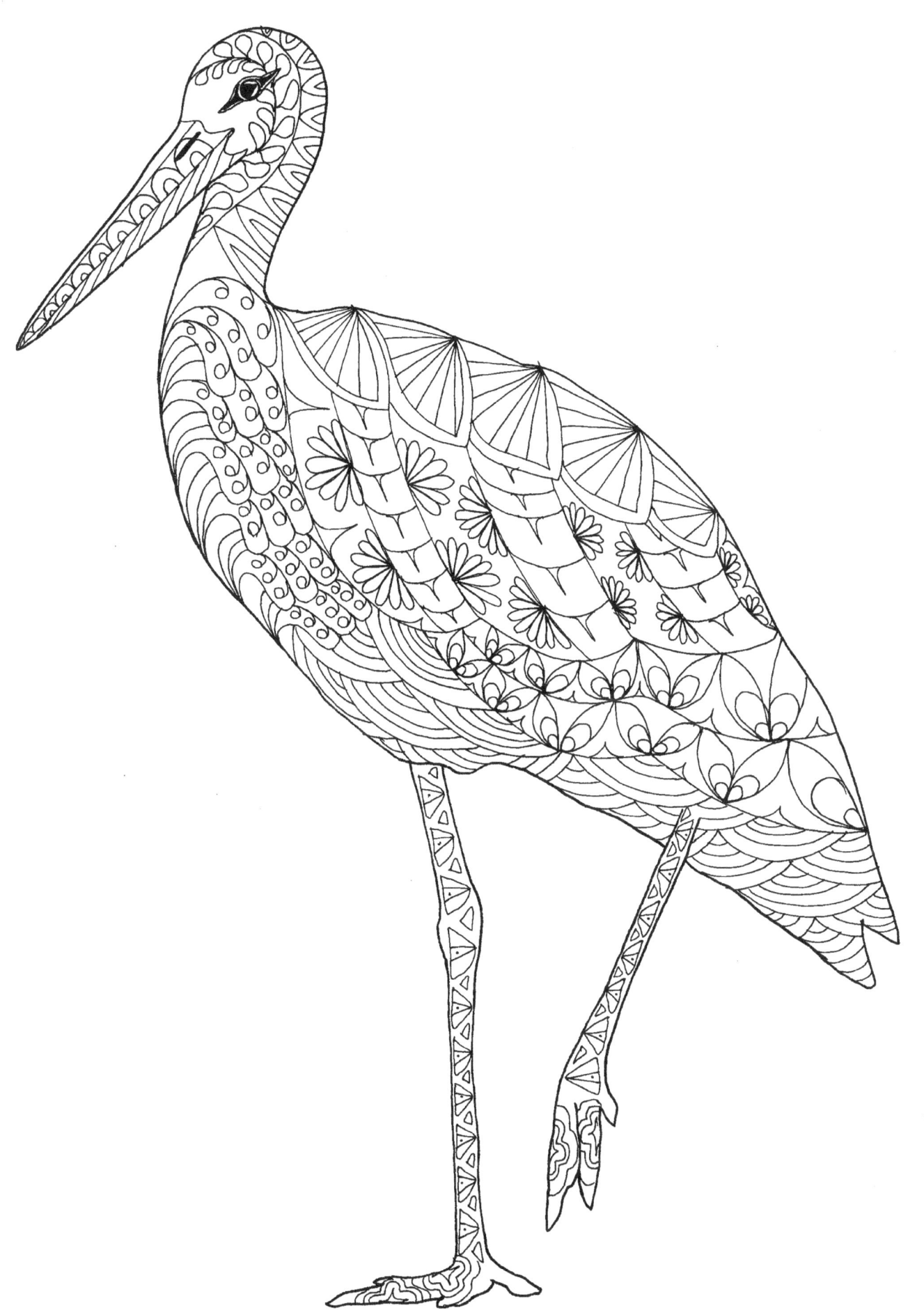

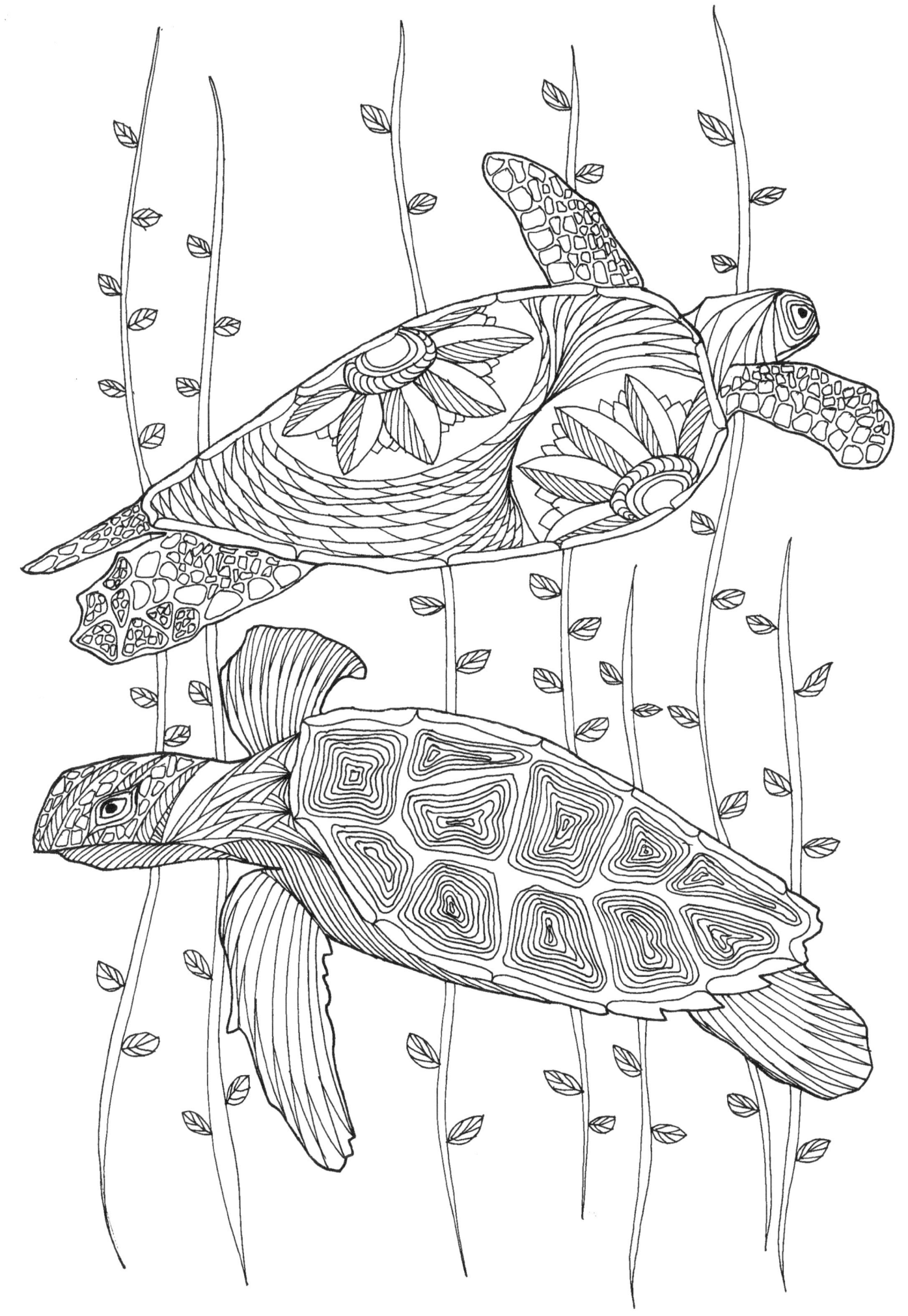

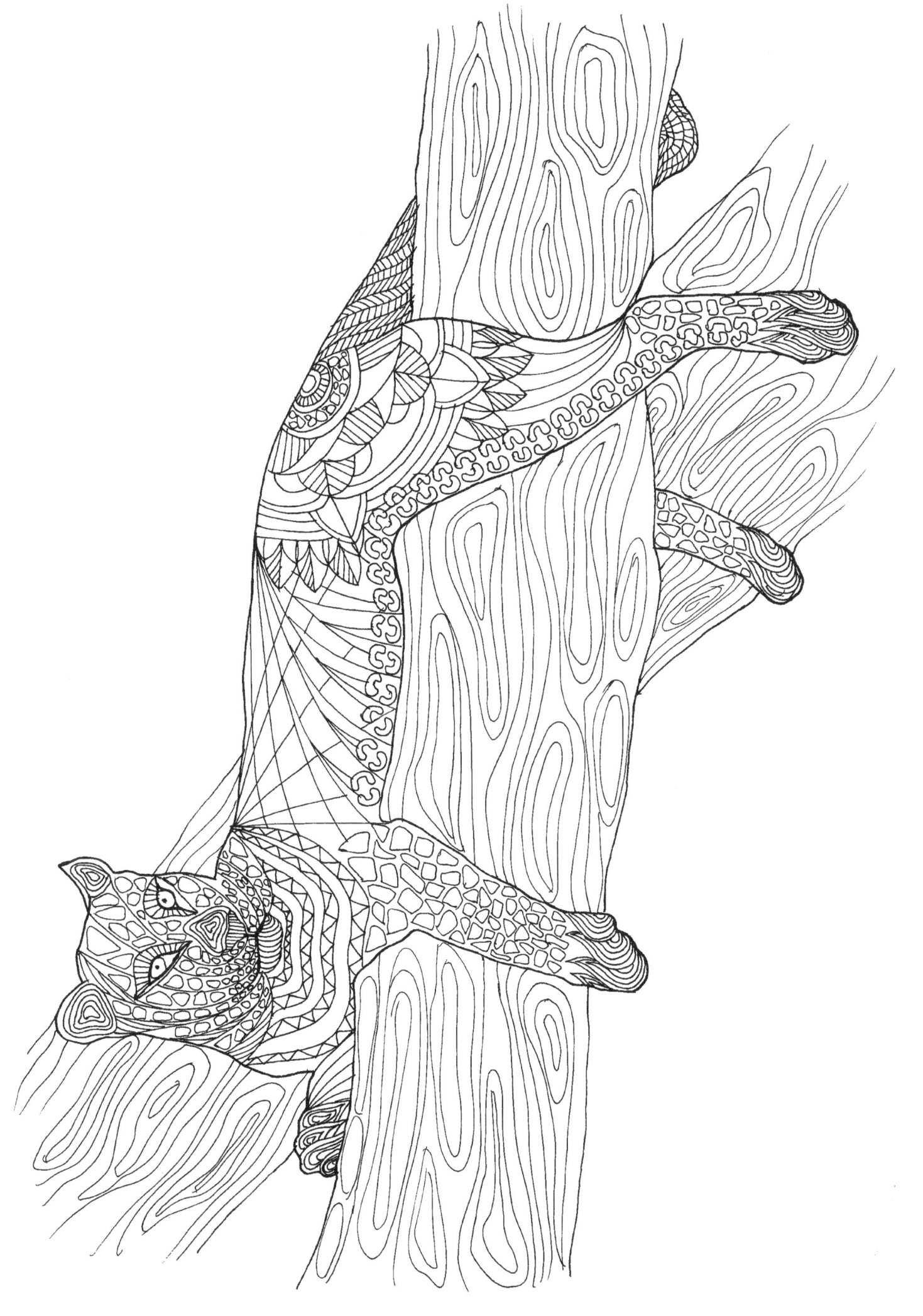

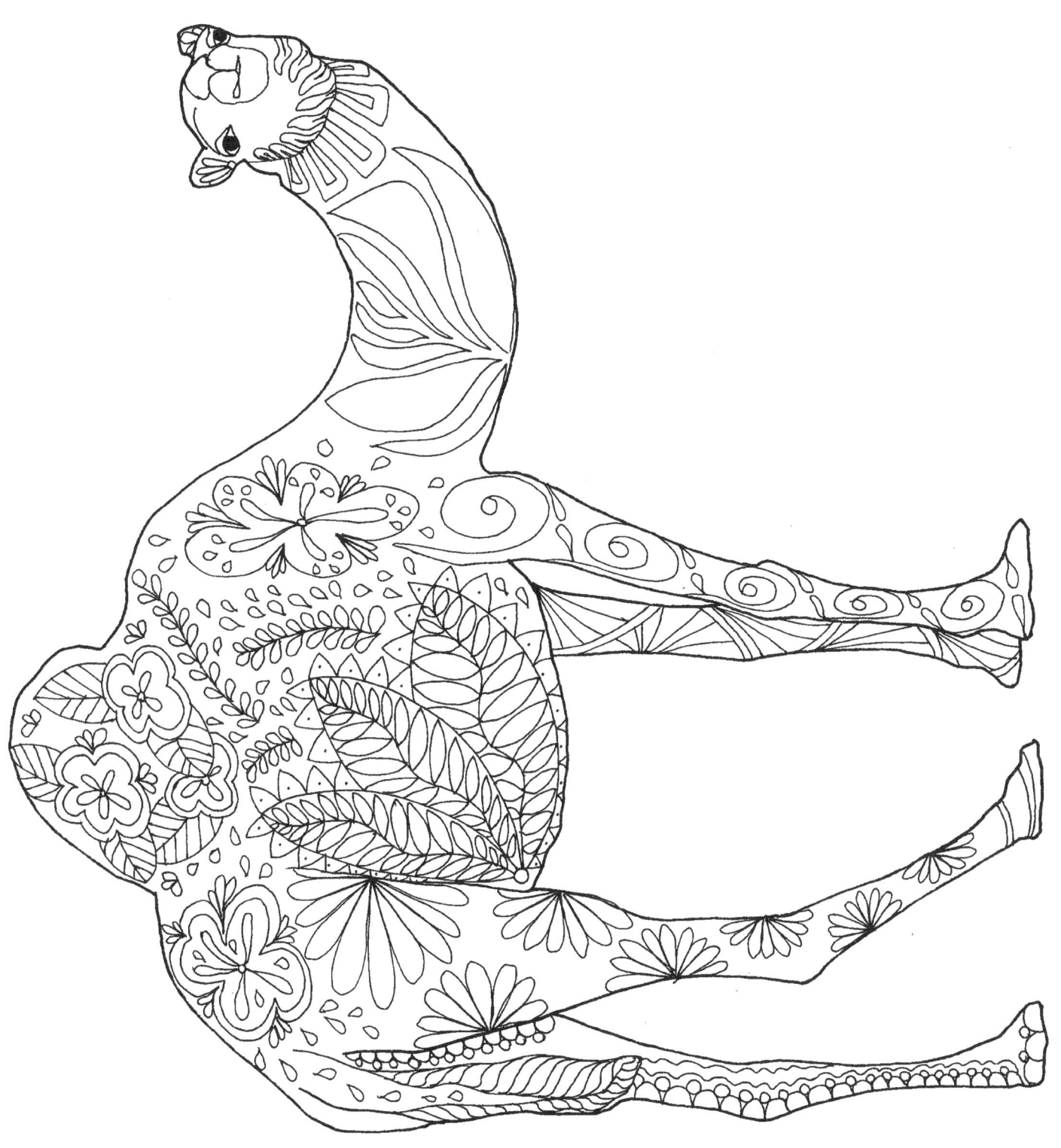

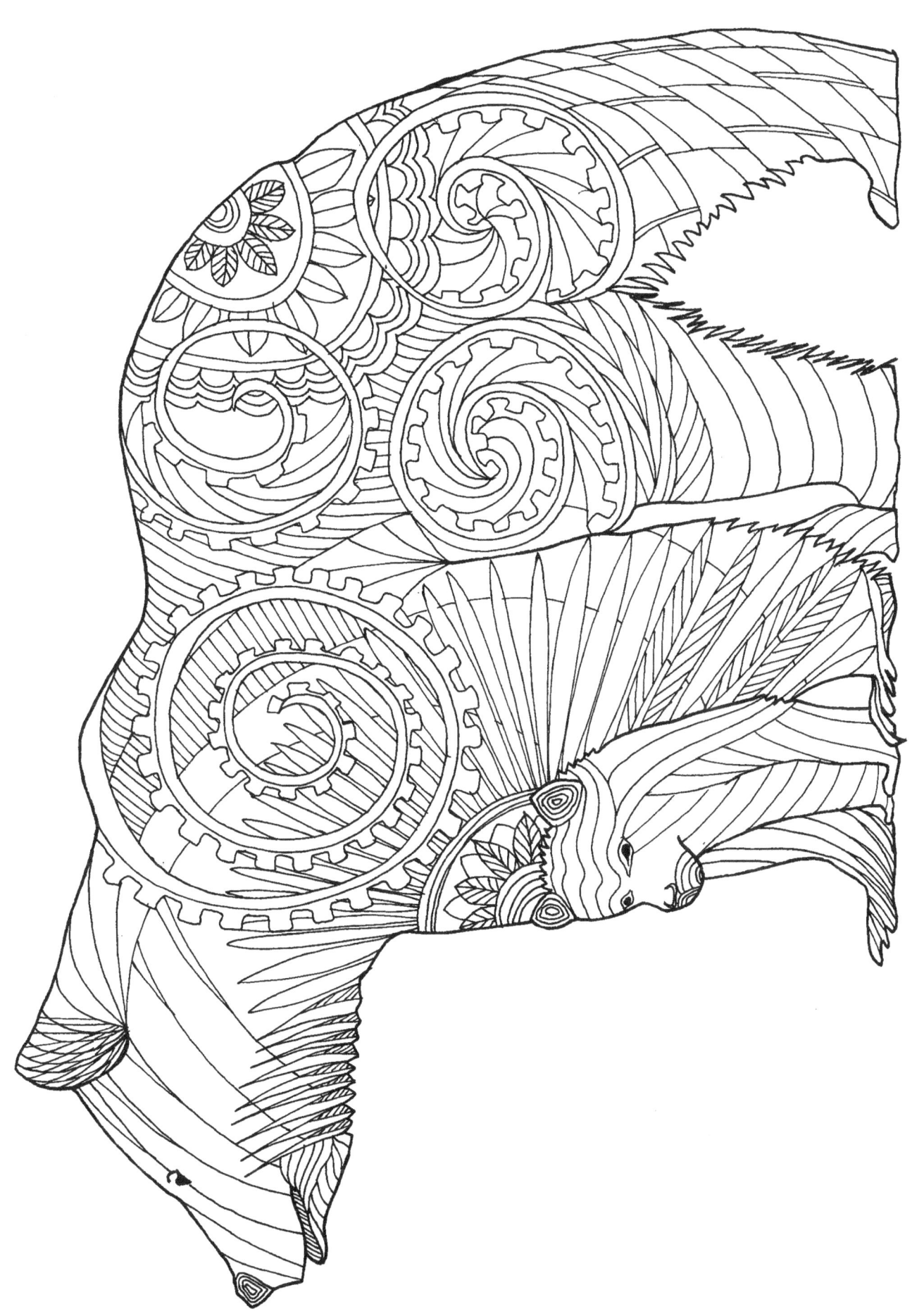

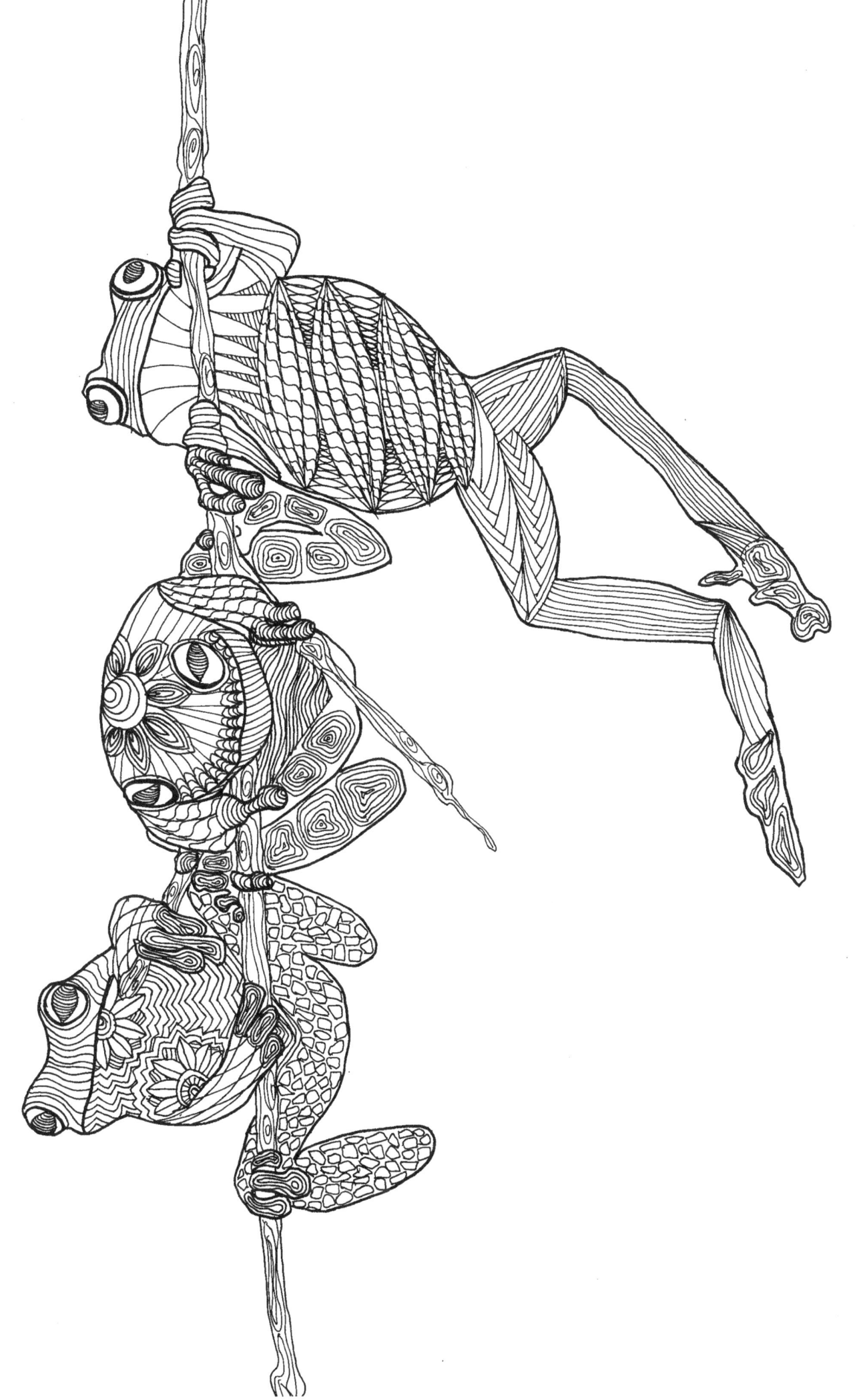

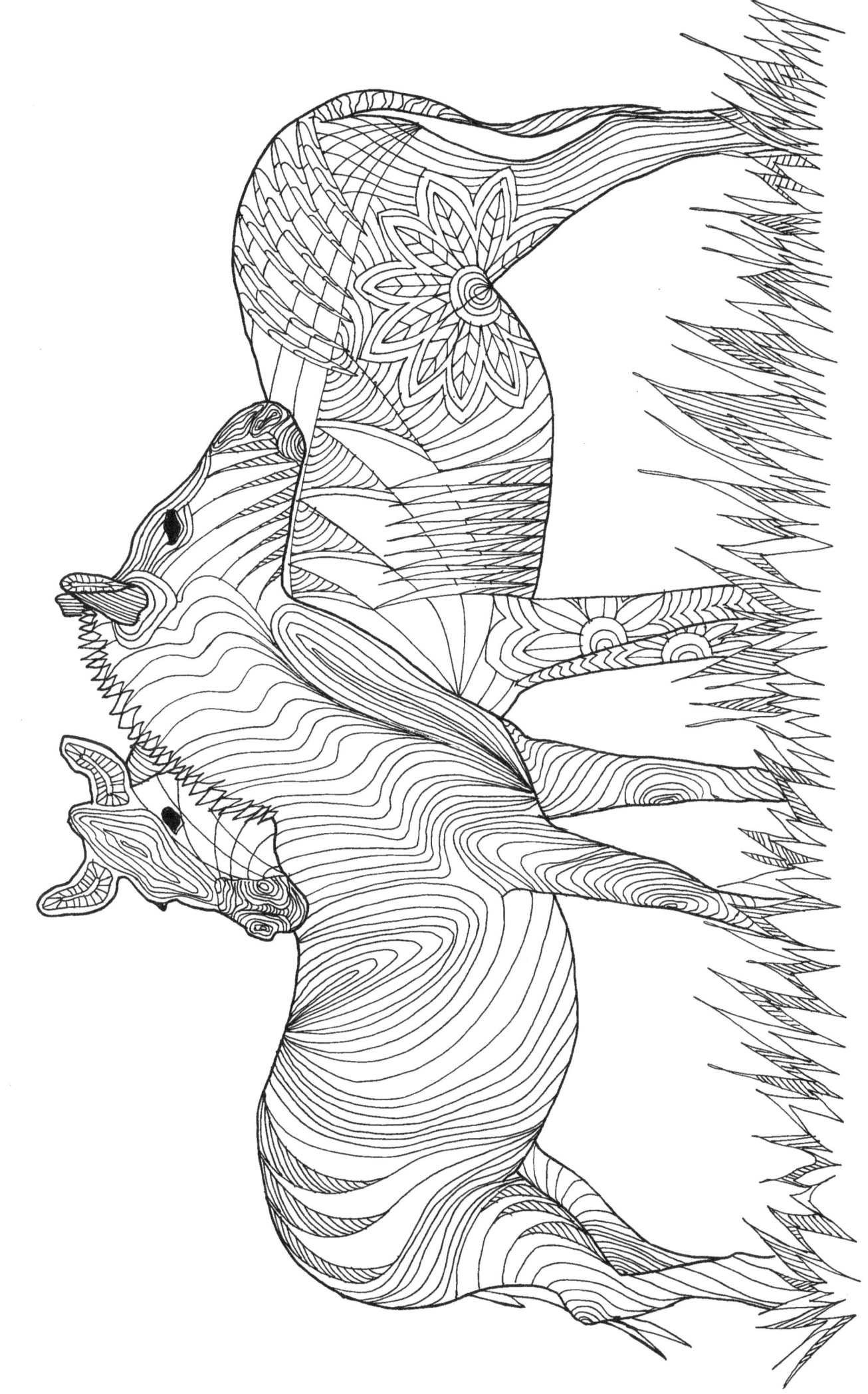

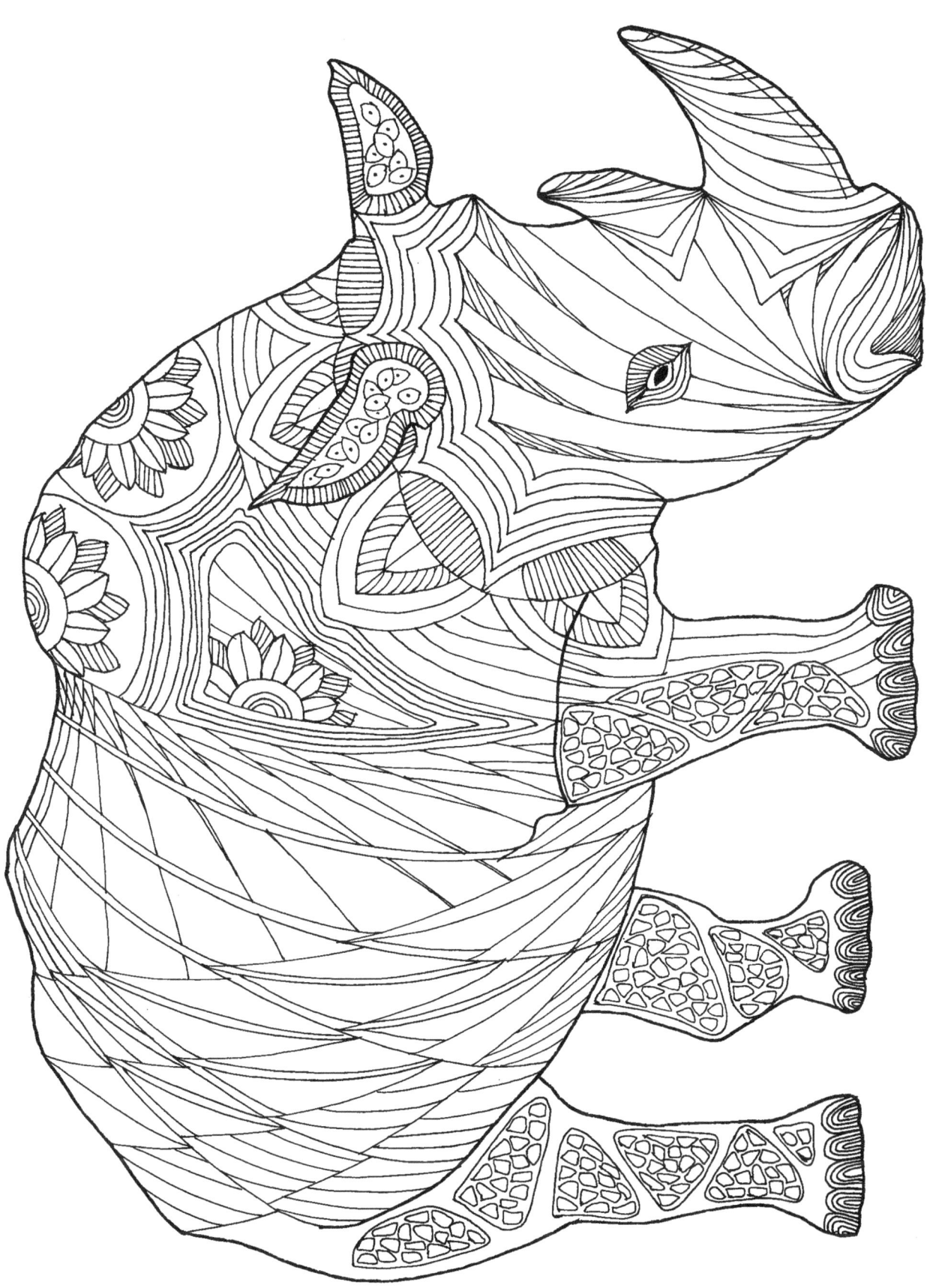

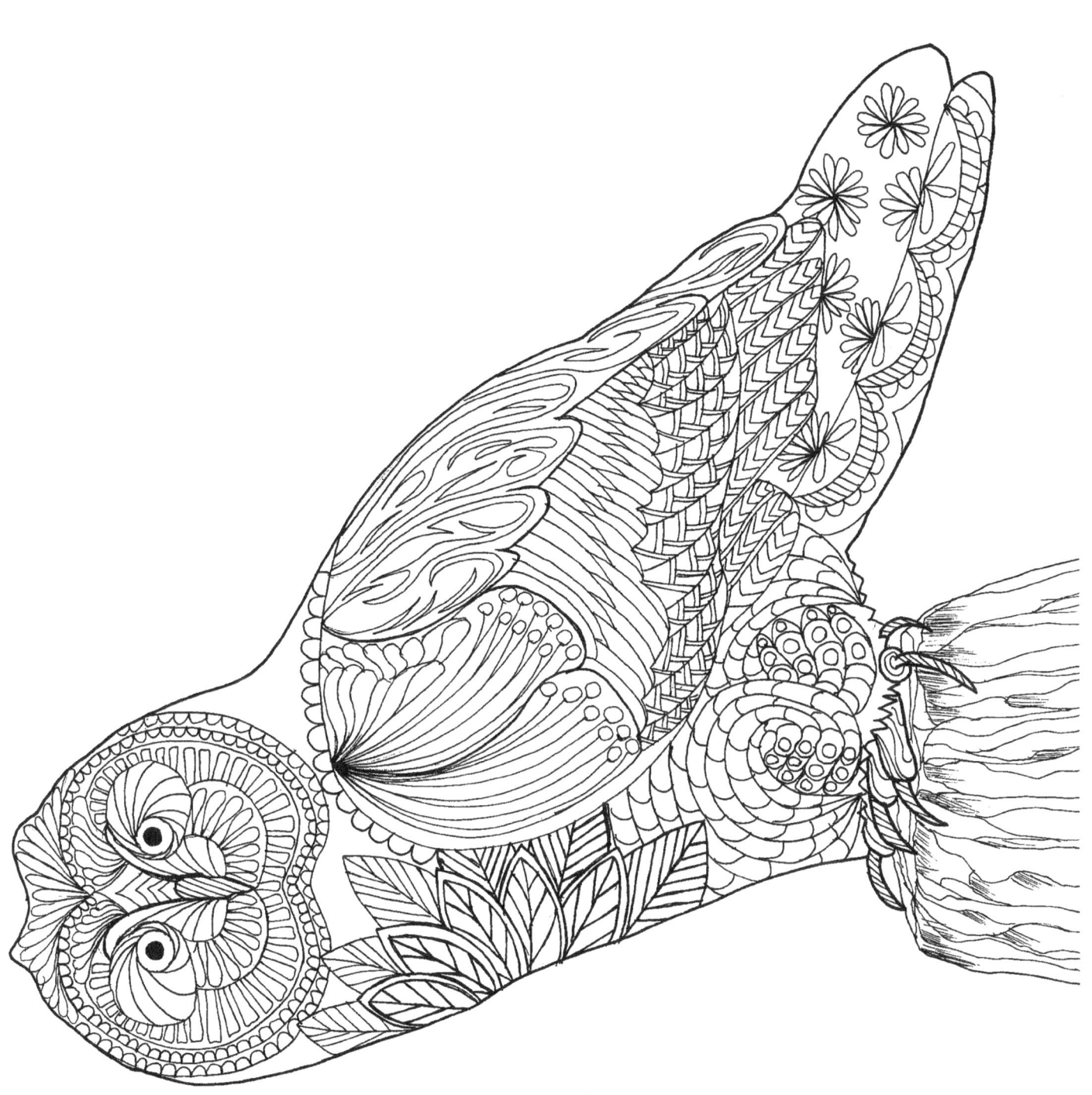

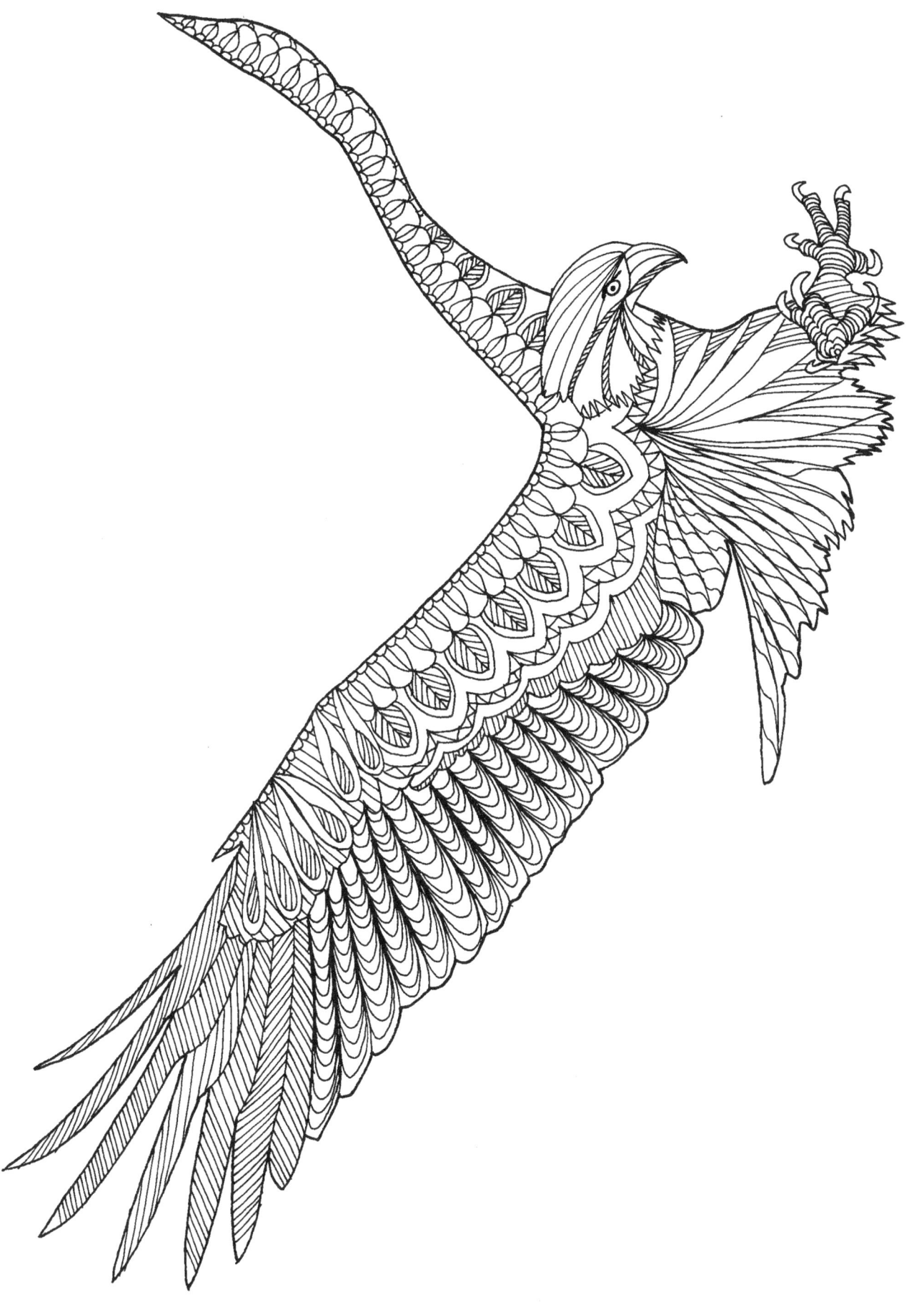

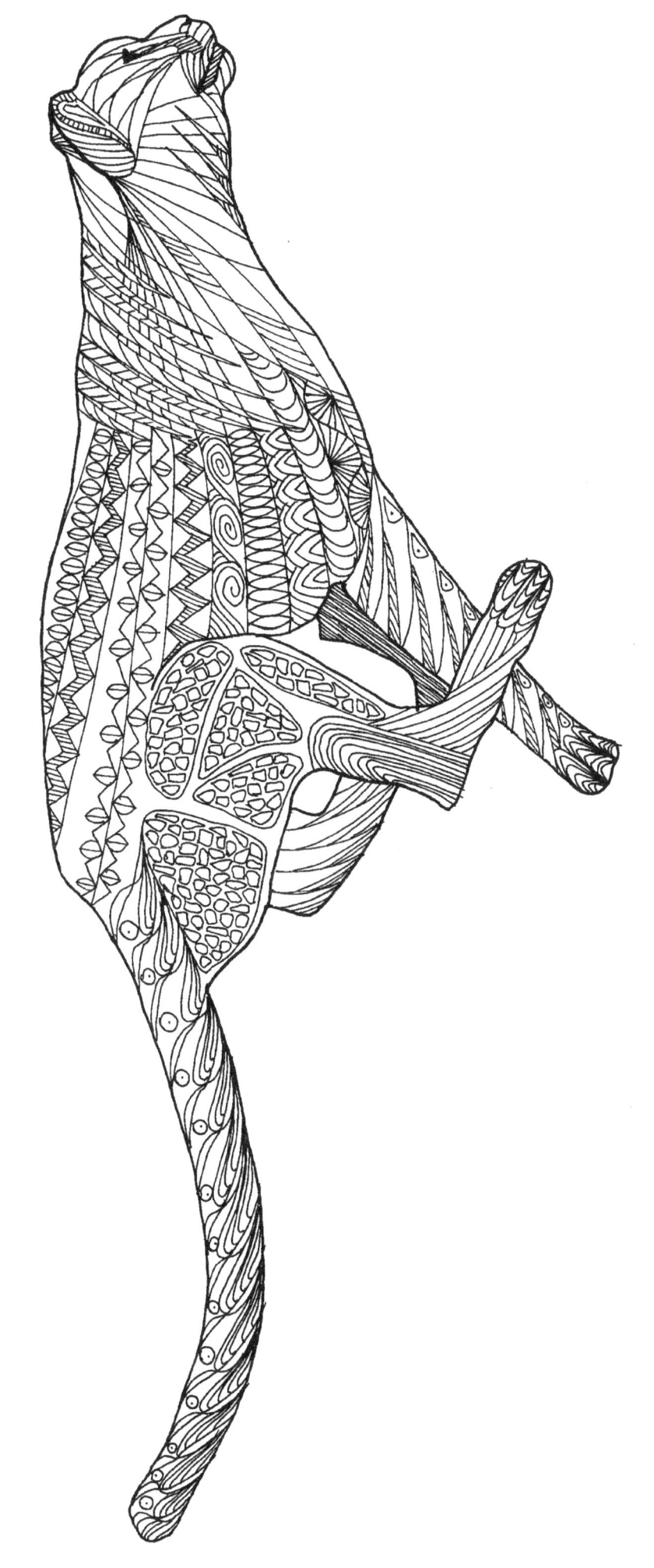

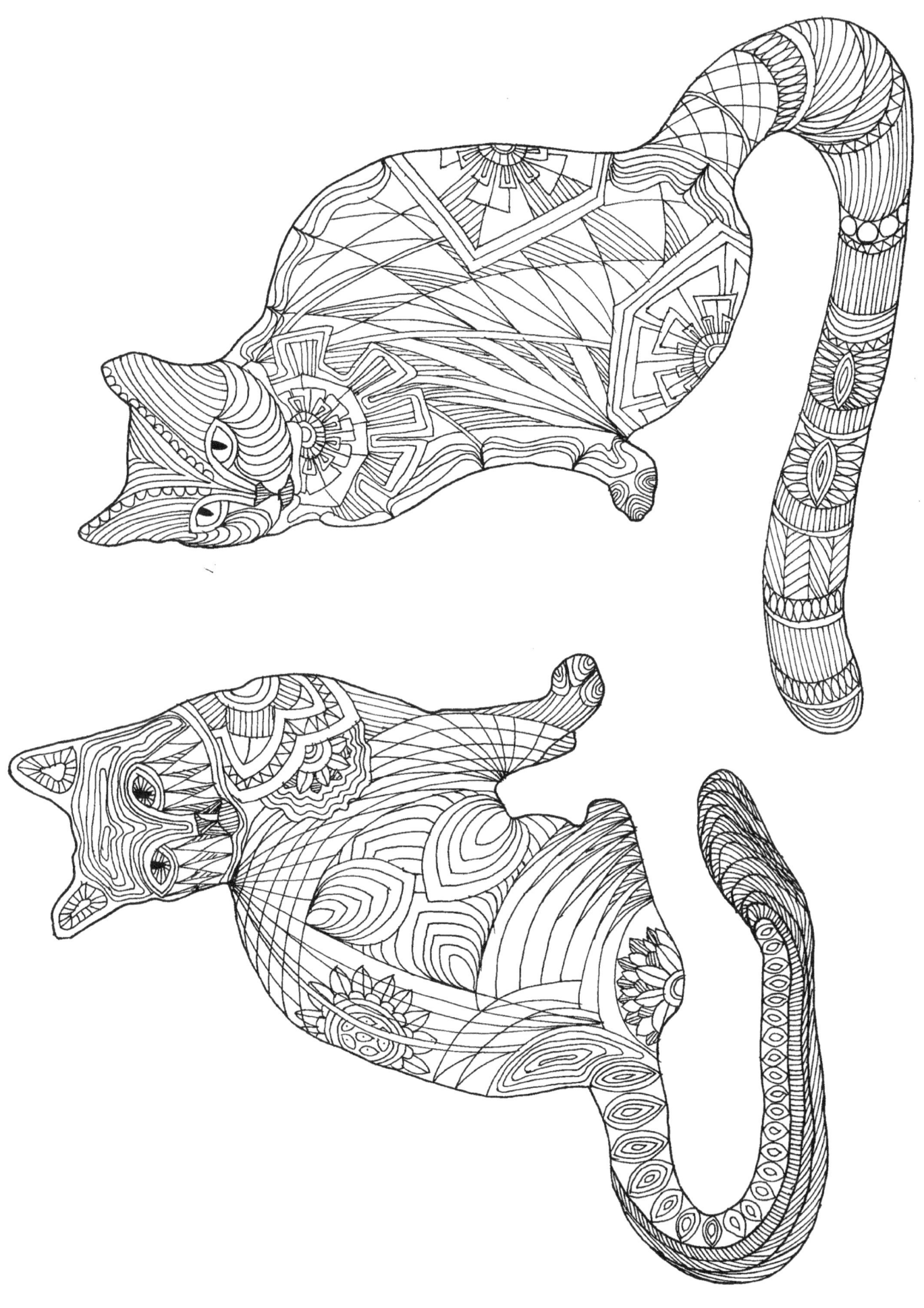

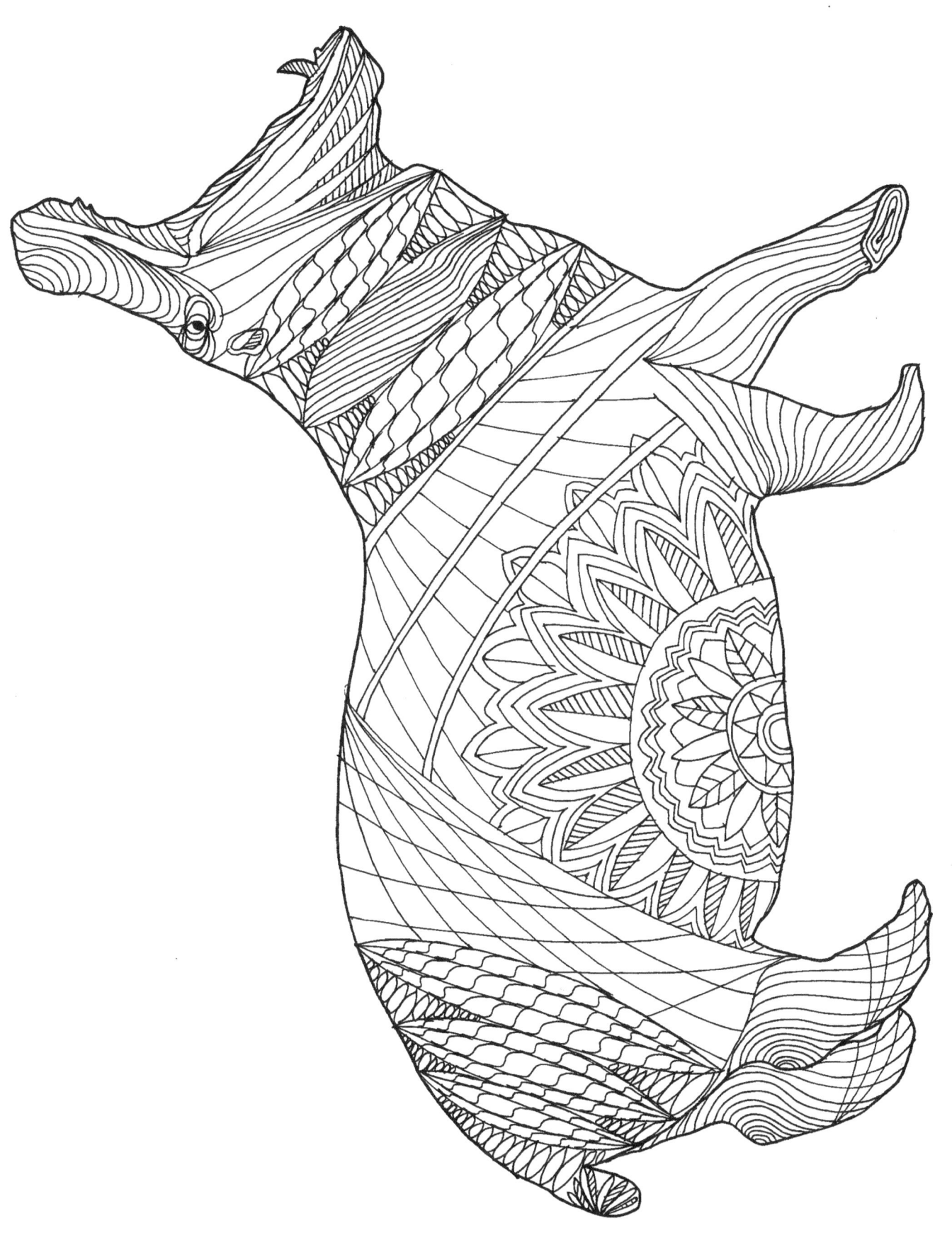

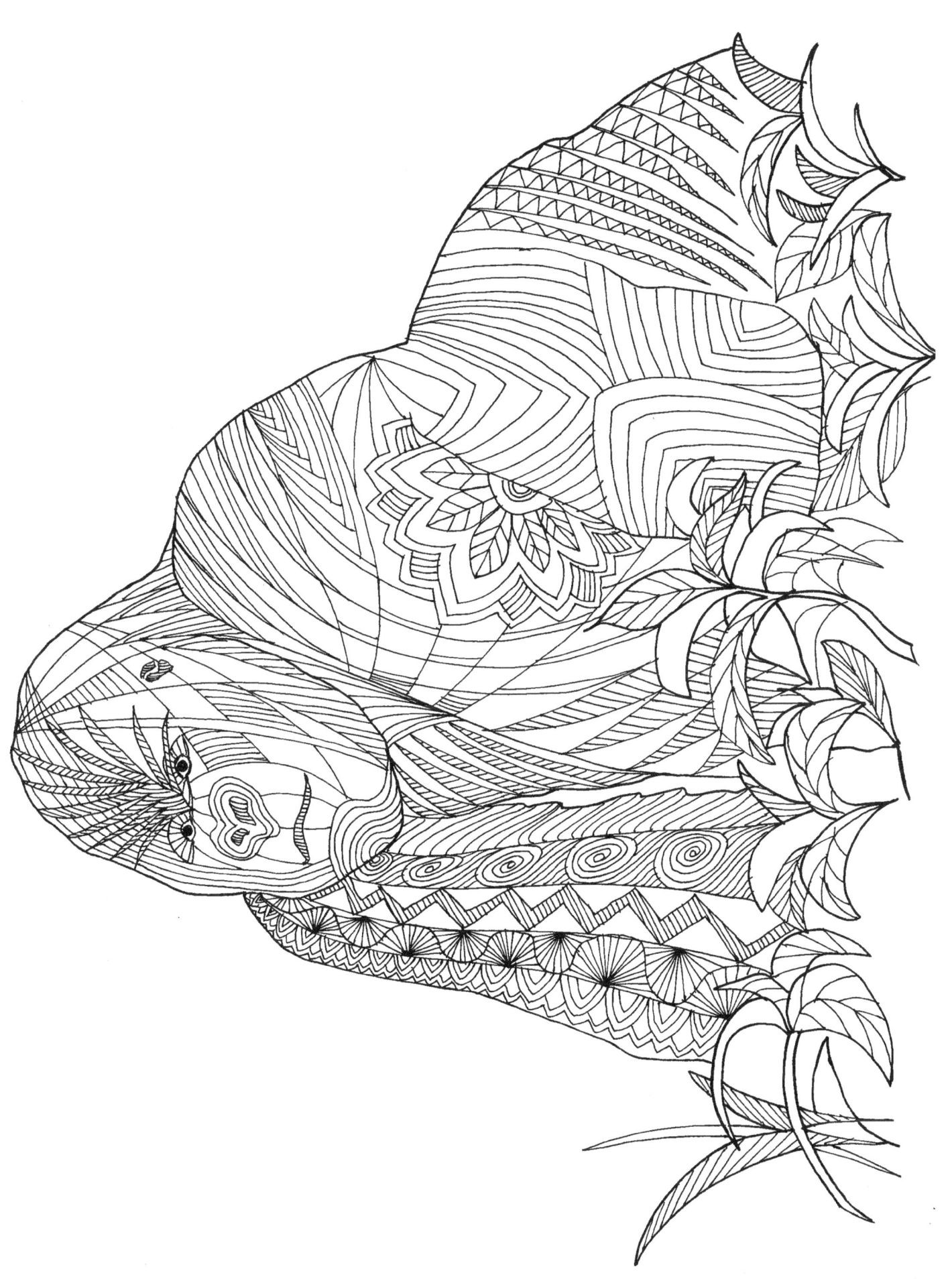

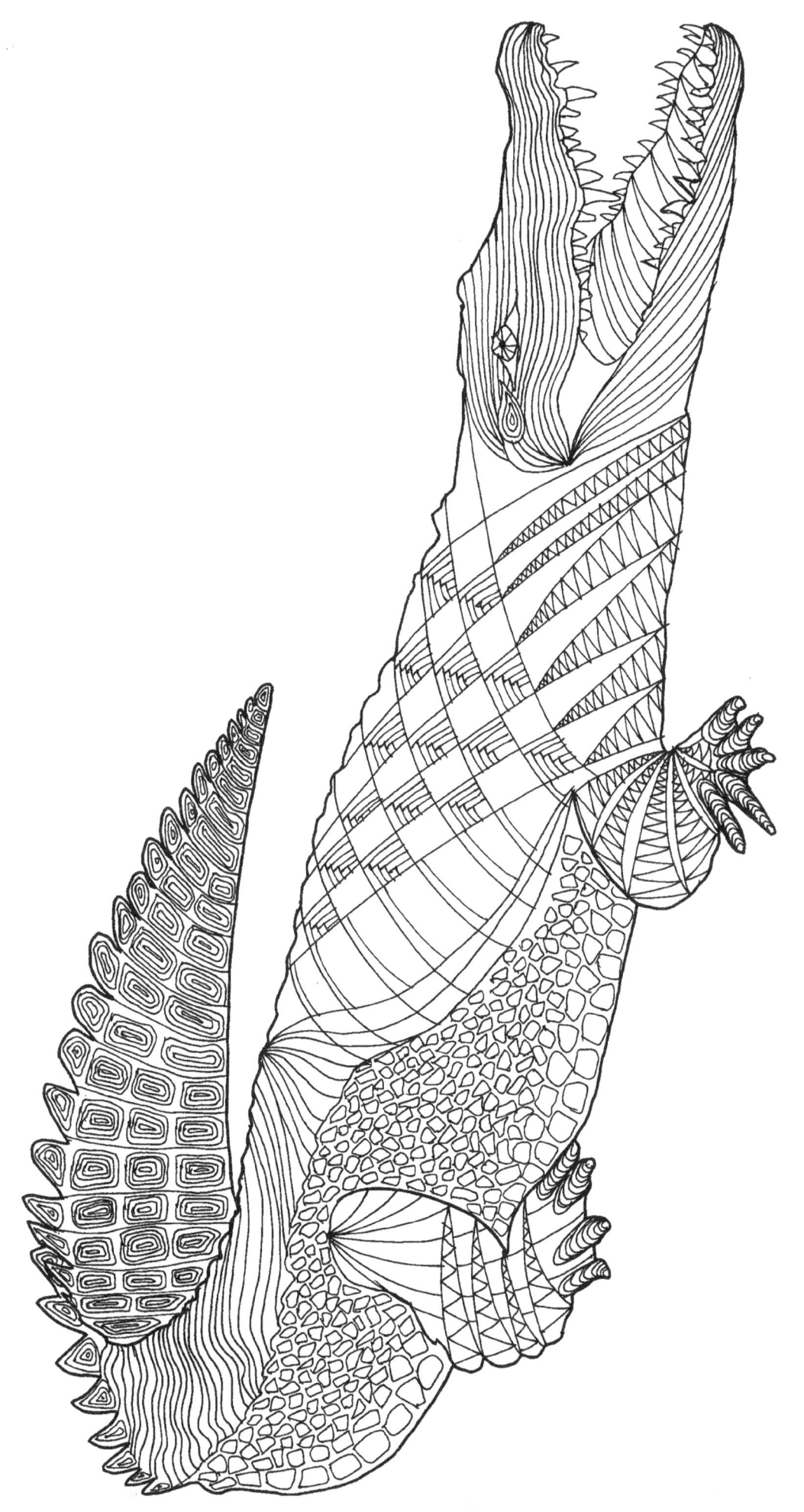

Be Happy Coloring Books

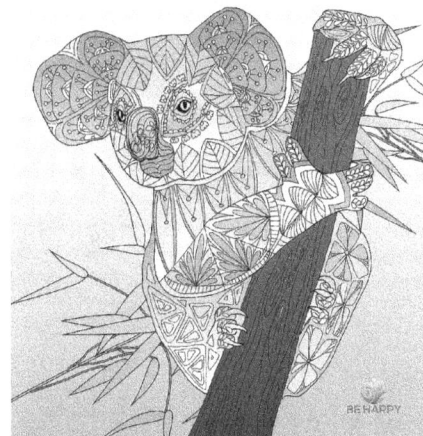

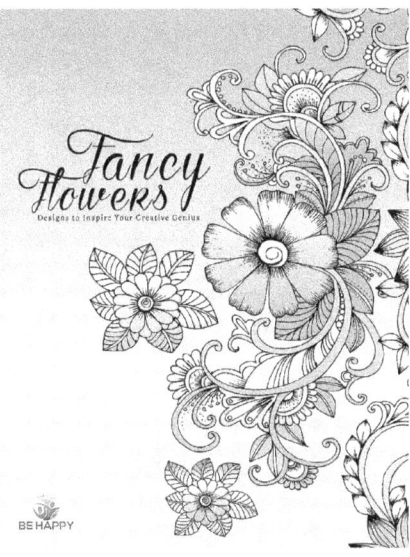

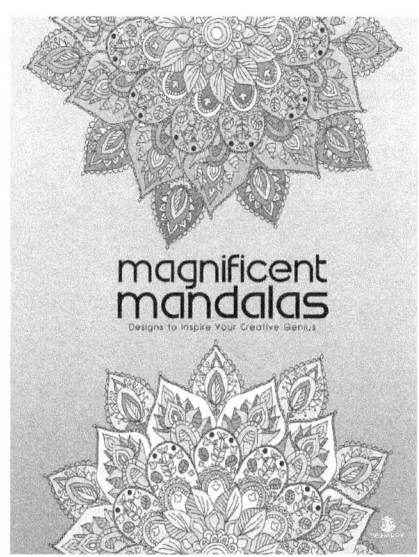

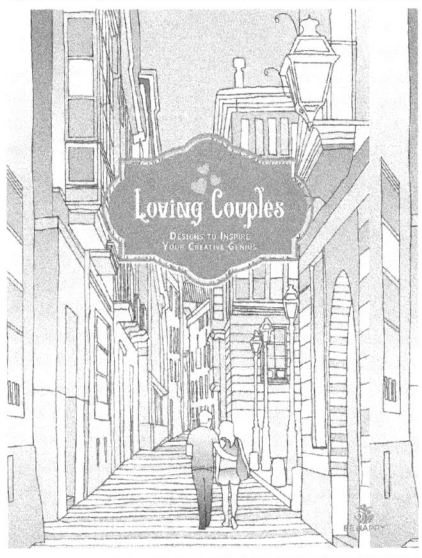

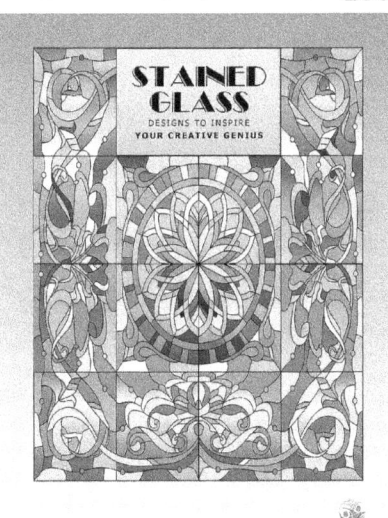

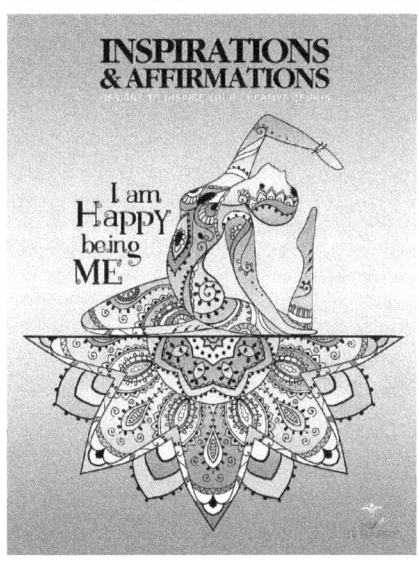

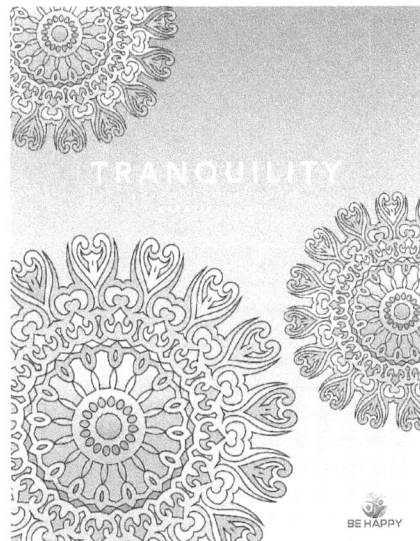

Stay tuned, more coloring books to come.
Our artists are passionately creating
new coloring pages to help inspire
your creative genius.

www.BeHappyColoringBooks.com

www.ingramcontent.com/pod-product-compliance
Lightning Source LLC
Chambersburg PA
CBHW080833170526
45158CB00009B/2558